STEVEN SPIELBERG

STEVEN SPIELBERG

From Reels to Riches
by Ted Gottfried

A Book Report Biography
FRANKLIN WATTS
A Division of Grolier Publishing
New York / London / Hong Kong / Sydney
Danbury, Connecticut

DEDICATION
For Tom Coakley, son-in-law par excellence
—Peace and Love

Cover illustration by Dave Klaboe,
interpreted from a photograph by © Sygma/Eric Robert

Frontispiece: Steven Spielberg at the New York Film Critics Circle
Awards on January 1, 1999

Photographs ©: AP/Wide World Photos: 110 (Chris Martinez);
Archive Photos: 107 (Gary Hershorn/Reuters), 2 (Victor Malafronte), 105
(Reuters/HO), 65; Corbis-Bettmann: 41 (Hulton-Deutsch Collection), 91
(Reuters), 23 (John Springer); Liaison Agency, Inc.: 17 (Barry King), 101
(Marc Rylewski), 11; Photofest: 96 (Andrew Cooper), 76 (Daily Mirror), 67
(Universal City Florida Partners), 46 (Universal Pictures), 71
(Warner Bros. Inc.), 9, 35, 60; Richard Y. Hoffman Jr.: 24; Seth Poppel
Yearbook Archives: 30; Sygma: 58 (D. Fineman), 80 (Stuart Franklin), 88
(David James), cover (Eric Robert), 82, 94.

Visit Franklin Watts on the Internet at:
http://publishing.grolier.com

Library of Congress Cataloging-in-Publication Data

Gottfried, Ted.
    Steven Spielberg : from reels to riches / by Ted Gottfried.
    Includes bibliographical references and index.
    Summary: Discusses the personal life and professional career of suc-
cessful filmmaker, Steven Spielberg.
    ISBN 0-531-11672-7   (lib. bdg.)   0-531-16493-4 (pbk.)
    1. Spielberg, Steven, 1947– —Juvenile literature 2. Motion picture
producers and directors—United States—Biography—Juvenile literature.
[1. Spielberg, Steven, 1947– 2. Motion picture producers and directors.] I.
Title. II. Series.
PN1998.3.S65 G68 2000
791.43'0233'092—dc21
        [B]   99-058477

CONTENTS

CHAPTER ONE

RECAPTURED IMAGES

The subconscious is the part of your mind that stores memories you don't realize you remember. They may be mere fragments—visions as fleeting as a flash card, pictures captured, stored, and forgotten in the blink of an eye. But these pictures, filed away in early childhood, sometimes reappear in people's minds later in life. Just such stored-up images became the raw material of the films of Steven Spielberg.

THE ARK AND THE LIGHT

One of Steven's earliest images came the day his father took him to the Adath Israel **synagogue.** At the end of a long corridor, the sacred scroll of the **Torah** was stored in a chest—a replica of the biblical Ark of the Covenant. The Ark was bathed in a reddish glow, which may have been sunlight.

That image, imprinted on Steven's brain, recurs in different ways in the movies he directs. "The movies I make have to pass through me before they get to the screen. I'm stuck with who I am," he has said. "I've always loved what I call 'God lights,' shafts coming out of the sky, or out of a spaceship, or coming through a doorway." In *Raiders of the Lost Ark,* sunlight shining through an amulet reveals the location of the Ark. In *Close Encounters of the Third Kind,* a small boy opens his front door and sees the ultra-bright, other-worldly light of an alien spacecraft. Candles illuminate the Sabbath service in *Schindler's List*: a blaze of light flickers down to one last, undying candle—a symbol of hope.

> "The movies I make have to pass through me before they get to the screen. I'm stuck with who I am."

HORROR, SNAKES, AND IMAGINARY PLAYMATES

Although hope is present in *Schindler's List,* so is horror. One of Steven's childhood memories came back to haunt him as an adult. He was three years old when he visited his grandmother in her home in Cincinnati, Ohio. At that time, a few years after

This shot from Close Encounters of the Third Kind *demonstrates Spielberg's visual trademark—light.*

the end of World War II (1941–1945), she had volunteered to teach English to concentration-camp survivors in her home. One of them showed Steven the tattoo number branded on his arm by the Nazis. The man twisted his arm this way and that to show Steven how the numeral 6 could be turned into a 9. Steven was too young then to understand the terror behind that tattoo, but years later, he conveyed the horror of the Holocaust to millions of moviegoers around the world.

When he was a small child, a very different sort of horrific vision imprinted itself on Steven's brain. He had been watching television when a

documentary about snakes came on. He couldn't take his eyes off the screen even though he became increasingly frightened. When the show was over, he was actually shaking with fear. For a long time afterward, Steven had nightmares about snakes. Years later, these nightmares were brought to the screen in *Raiders of the Lost Ark*. When Indiana Jones survives being thrown into a pit of snakes, he shudders with loathing and snarls, "I hate snakes!"

Not all of Steven's childhood imaginings were scary, though. He recalls a crack in the wall of his bedroom through which the hallway light shone. He put himself to sleep thinking up different kinds of small creatures who might live beyond the light in the crack. He pictured them as friendly creatures, and sometimes he imagined that they were urging him to come through the crack into the light and play with them. They were other-worldly—not pretty or cuddly—but more like playful lizards or turtles. Ultimately, this vision took shape in the form of *E.T. the Extra-Terrestrial*, which captured the hearts of film audiences around the world.

CREATING FEAR

As a child, however, most of Steven's imaginary creations were scary. At a young age, he developed the knack of casting hand shadows on the ceiling to create imaginary creatures. Most of these were monsters of one sort or another. Steven liked to scare himself with ghosts, goblins, dragons, and multi-tentacled Martians. These shadow creatures inspired scenes in the 1982 horror movie *Poltergeist,* which was based upon Steven's original story.

It was a short step from the thrill of scaring himself to the excitement of scaring others. For instance, there was the time young Steven saw a movie about Martians invading Earth. The Martians had octopus-like limbs and round heads that lit up. The combination made seven-year-old Steven's heart pound. After the movie, Steven

Spielberg, with his mother, Leah (center), and three sisters, Nancy, Sue, and Anne (left to right)

constructed a human skull from the contents of a plastic kit he had been given for his birthday. He put goggles over the empty eye sockets and topped it with the aviator cap his father had worn in the Army Air Force. Steven put a small light bulb inside the skull so that red rays of light shot out of the eye sockets. He propped the skull up against one wall of a dark, walk-in closet. He then blindfolded his three younger sisters, urged them to go inside the closet, and locked the door behind them. When they took off the blindfolds, they saw the skull and panicked. This incident became the basis for a scene in *Poltergeist*.

Terrorizing his sisters didn't quite satisfy Steven's early desire to entertain people, though. He had a larger vision of creatures much bigger than a skull in a closet. He had been to museums and seen dinosaurs. He had also seen *King Kong* and other old films on television in which such creatures played a major and terrifying role.

"I've had a fascination with dinosaurs all my life," he later told author Michael Crichton. In 1993, Spielberg directed the dinosaur-filled film version of Crichton's best-selling book, *Jurassic Park*.

VISIONS OF WAR

Many films about World War II were shown in the 1950s and early 1960s when Steven was growing up. These were patriotic years, and the actors who "died" in the movies did so bravely and willingly for their country. The action was all clear-cut—good guys against bad guys, bravery before self-preservation. Steven loved these heroic movies. For a long time, they blotted out another picture of the war—the one described by his father and his father's wartime buddies.

Arnold Spielberg had enlisted in the U.S. Army Air Force in World War II. He had flown as a radio operator in a squadron of B-25s known as the "Burma Bridge Busters." Throughout Steven's childhood, his father talked about the war. Often, he held reunions with other members of his squadron in the Spielberg home. At the reunions, Steven got a realistic, scary impression of war instead of the heroic picture presented in Hollywood movies. According to the veterans, bravery came second to the desire to survive. The veterans described their experiences as confusing, and their memories were cruel and painful.

"I chose to believe the war movies instead of my dad and his friends because their stories were so horrendously harsh," Spielberg admits. Over time, however, these opposing images of war fused in Spielberg's mind, combining patriotism and the reality of war. The result of these fused images is *Saving Private Ryan*, which some critics consider to be Spielberg's greatest film.

THE SPIELBERG PERSPECTIVE

At some point in his childhood, probably without his being aware of it, Steven's mind had switched from merely thinking about images to create on film to actually creating them. The Spielberg technique was developing. It was on the ceiling when he made shadow pictures, and it was there in the closet with the red-eyed skull. But the first real indication of "the Spielberg touch" came when he got his hands on the 8-mm movie camera his mother had given his father for Father's Day.

Steven's mother and father were leaving on vacation, and they asked Steven to take a picture of their camper leaving the driveway. Steven stretched out on his stomach and aimed the camera at the hubcap. As his parents wondered what he was doing, Steven pulled back so that the spinning hubcap turned into the whole camper.

Instinctively, Steven had created the connection between the wheel in motion and the start of the trip. He had applied the tool most necessary to a film director—**perspective**—and he had used it in a unique way. As he grew up, his perspective became Steven's trademark.

Many years later, he filmed *Saving Private Ryan* "from three, four, or five inches off the sand and dirt so I wouldn't get my head blown off." Spielberg adds, "The battles are shot from the point of view of a combat soldier, not a Hollywood director." The result was a depiction of the D-Day landings that critics have called the most realistic battle **footage** ever shot. This scene and the critical acclaim it has received illustrate the power of Spielberg's perspective.

Saving Private Ryan and *Schindler's List* show that the childhood pictures in Spielberg's head are much more than just the fantastic imaginings in *E.T.* and *Jurassic Park*. These recaptured images show that he can fashion reality out of real-life images. They have moved him beyond mere entertainment to visions that strike at the heart. They reveal a film director as many-sided as he is talented.

This is the story of that director.

CHAPTER TWO

A DIRECTOR IS BORN

When Steven Spielberg first became famous, he told interviewers that he was born on December 18, 1947, in Cincinnati, Ohio. Actually, he had been born a year earlier, on December 18, 1946. Many people still believe that he was born in 1947. Spielberg has never given any reason for the discrepancy. Only a white lie—more peculiar than serious—it was probably intended to confirm his image as a boy genius who made his first movie before the age of twenty-one.

FATHER AND MOTHER

Steven Allan Spielberg was the first child and only son of Arnold Spielberg and Leah Posner Spielberg. They were both from Cincinnati, Ohio. They had met there and married during World War II. All four of Arnold and Leah's parents were Jewish immigrants who had fled turn-of-the-cen-

Spielberg and his father, Arnold

tury persecution in Poland and Austria.

After World War II, Arnold Spielberg's electronics skills involved him in the early development of computers. This led to an offer from RCA, and he moved his family to Haddon Township, New Jersey, in August 1952. Steven's earliest memories of his father are of a tinkerer and workaholic who brought home strange gadgetry to work on. He often ignored his children.

Leah, Steven's mother, had been trained to be

a concert pianist. Marriage, however, put an end to her musical career. She was a small woman who moved quickly and smoothly, but she was inclined to be nervous and sometimes fearful. She was terrified of flying and passed this fear on to her son. She also passed her love of music on to him.

WILD ANIMALS AND PEANUT BUTTER

A year or so after his family moved to Haddon Township, Steven was taken to the movies for the first time. The picture was *The Greatest Show on Earth,* Cecil B. DeMille's Oscar-winning, Technicolor extravaganza about the circus. Little Steven was thoroughly captivated by the spectacle of wild animals, flying trapezes, and best of all, the sensational train crash at the **climax** of the film. It was his first experience sitting before a screen that somehow seemed bigger than life.

Steven's imagination took off from that movie and from others he saw during his early childhood. He was a boy who lived in his mind more than in his body. He was thin, uncoordinated, and a poor athlete. When teams were chosen for stickball or touch football, he was often the last one picked. Aware of his shortcomings and sensitive to criticism, Steven withdrew more and more, spending hours behind his closed bedroom door. There, his fantasies roamed freely.

Steven had a mischievous side and played many childhood pranks, such as coating a neighbor's windows with peanut butter. His mother remembers that Steven's "badness was so original that there weren't even books to tell you what to do."

THE CLIFFHANGER INFLUENCE

When Steven was given an electric train set, his chief joy became re-creating the train crash in *The Greatest Show on Earth*. At the same time, he became fascinated by the old movies shown on TV during those early days of television. Without realizing it, he was absorbing the styles and techniques of such early directors as John Ford *(Stagecoach),* Frank Capra *(Lost Horizon),* and James Whale *(Frankenstein).*

Like many children of his generation, Steven went to the movies on Saturday afternoons. The main attraction was the **serials**—filmed adventure stories split up into fifteen- to twenty-minute episodes with **cliffhanger** endings. Each week, the hero—Captain Marvel, Tailspin Tommy, or Commander Cody—was left dangling at death's door only to be saved at the beginning of the episode shown on the following week. Speeding trucks, dynamited buildings, death rays, and deadly poisons would threaten the heroes. Then they were rescued and proven indestructible. The certain-death and superhuman survival pattern of these serials later became the basis for the sequences in *Raiders of the Lost Ark* and the two *Indiana Jones* movies that followed.

"THE RETARD"

In 1957, Steven's father accepted a job with General Electric and moved his family to Phoenix, Arizona. Those years in Arizona were not happy ones for him. In junior high school, he remembers being "the weird, skinny kid with acne." Steven's lack of ability at sports, combined with his poor showing in class, prompted classmates to call him "the retard."

His mother recalls, "He wasn't a good student. He was less than mediocre. He needed tutors in French and math." To seal his fate as "the retard," he threw up in biology class while dissecting a frog. (This experience later became the basis for a scene in *E.T.*)

EXPANDING HIS HORIZONS

Things weren't altogether bleak for Steven, however. As soon as he showed an interest in anything—puppets, trains, the clarinet, even birds—his parents supplied whatever was necessary to encourage that interest. His three younger sisters—Anne, Sue, and Nancy—took their lead from their parents and also indulged Steven. They appeared in the skits he wrote, fetched and carried for his hobbies, and allowed him to terrify them with the monsters he created.

When he entered Arcadia High School in Phoenix in 1961, Steven's life outside the home improved. By then he had joined a Boy Scout troop. On camping trips, his storytelling skills earned the admiration of other scouts and leaders. Richard Hoffman, leader of Troop 294, recalls, "Stevie would start telling his ghost stories, and everyone would suddenly get quiet so they could all hear it." Later, he was elected to the Boy Scouts honor society—the Order of the Arrow— and he became an Eagle Scout.

Steven also got involved in school activities. He took up the clarinet and eventually played in the school band. He joined the Arcadia Theatre Arts Program. Steven directed *Guys and Dolls* for the program.

A CAREER BEGINS

When Steven was twelve years old, he had become interested in filmmaking. The movies Arnold Spielberg made with his 8-mm camera disappointed his son. After years of watching movies on TV, Steven was sensitive to bad **framing** and **composition,** lack of continuity, jerky camera handling, and **overexposed** film. He pointed out these faults to his father. Finally, Arnold handed him the camera and told him to do better if he could.

Steven photographed his electric trains crashing with inventive special effects. He threw bags of flour into the air to create clouds of smoke for explosions. He overboiled a cherry dessert in a pressure cooker so that he could film the remains—blood-like red glop. He wrote little three-minute skits and bullied his sisters into acting in them. He was a painstaking director, and he would reduce his sisters to tears until he had the scene on film just the way he wanted it. When the family went camping, Steven shot their tent-raising, their campfire meals, their midday swims, and their berry-picking. He directed their every movement, sometimes driving his parents and sisters into a frustrated fury. His hobby was a form of escape. Spielberg admits, "When I didn't want to face the real world, I just stuck a camera up to my face."

> **"When I didn't want to face the real world, I just stuck a camera up to my face."**

THE FIRST STORY LINE

It wasn't long before Steven persuaded his parents to trade up for a better camera with a three-

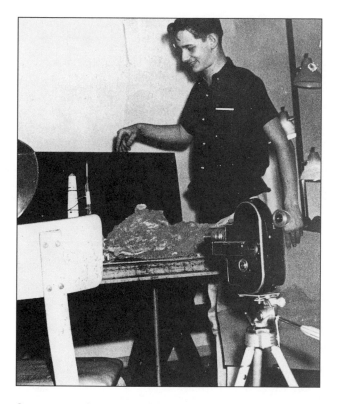

Steven makes one of his many amateur films.

lens **turret.** This allowed him to take close-ups and **long and medium shots,** and he could also **cut** from one to the other for dramatic effect. He joined a Boy Scout photography program and set about making his first movie to earn a merit badge. A fellow scout put on a cowboy suit, and Steven transformed him into an outlaw robbing a

Steven, with his camera and fellow Boy Scout
Ray Cheehall in July 1961

stagecoach. Only three minutes long, the film built to a climax in which the outlaw—with an appropriately evil leer—counts his stolen money. Steven eventually called the movie *Gunsmog*—a takeoff on the popular television series "Gunsmoke."

Filming and developing these mini-movies cost money. Steven's parents were generous, but they had their limits. So, Steven decided to turn the family den into a makeshift theater to get the money. He charged twenty-five cents admission, sold refreshments, and showed movies to classmates.

Sometimes he rented films, such as *Davy Crockett, King of the Wild Frontier*, and *War of the Worlds*. Sometimes he put together programs of short films he had shot himself. These were popular because he used some of his classmates as actors. Even those who weren't in the films enjoyed seeing those who were, and there was much laughing, hooting, and jeering at their performances.

FIRELIGHT

During his Arizona school years, Steven made some fifteen films with stories. The most ambitious one was called *Firelight*. He wrote the **script** himself in early 1963. It was about aliens who invade Earth and steal an entire city. They take it apart and put it together again on their home planet.

Working weekends, it took Steven a year—filming from June to December 1963—to make *Firelight*. He even persuaded a local airport to close off a runway for him so that he could shoot one sequence. Despite his youth, he talked a local hospital into letting him shoot on its premises. The Arizona desert provided the landscape for the alien planet.

Steven **edited** the film himself. His father paid $400 to hire a local theater to show it, and in March 1964, all of the Spielbergs leaned on friends and relatives, scouts and schoolmates to attend the premiere. The film was a sellout, netting $100 profit on Arnold Spielberg's investment.

In 1964, after the showing of *Firelight*, Arnold accepted an offer to join IBM as a computer consultant in Saratoga, California, and the family had to move immediately. This sudden and wrenching move marked a major change in Steven's life.

CHAPTER THREE

THE BUMPY ROAD TO MOVIELAND

"Hey, Jewboy!" The taunt echoed through the halls of the high school in Saratoga, California. Steven felt as if he had been plunged into a world of **anti-Semitic** bullies. They sneezed, "Hah-Jew," when they walked past him in the halls, and they flung pennies at him. "Every penny sounded like the explosion of a bazooka," he remembers. "Pick them up, Jew!" they snarled.

The kick-in-the-guts feeling of their hatred stayed with Steven all his life. The memory filled him with frustrated rage. The same rage was there when he filmed *Schindler's List*.

JEWISH IDENTITY

Being Jewish had been no big deal for Steven before he moved to Saratoga. His parents observed the Jewish holidays and some of the customs, but they were not particularly religious. They did not attend synagogue services regularly, and Steven and his sisters received no religious training. Steven never really thought of himself in terms of his Jewish identity.

His treatment by young anti-Semites brought that identity home to him, however. His first reaction was to back away from it. He didn't *feel* Jewish. It wasn't fair! He resented being defined as a Jew rather than as an individual. Steven had doubts about his self-worth, and he went through a phase of wondering if being Jewish was the reason for his failings.

That phase was short-lived, and it was replaced by fury. The anti-Semitic teenagers acted in gangs, and Steven was only one Jew with no way to fight back. So he kept quiet, held his head high, and took the persecution that came his way. All the time, he seethed with anger (which he didn't allow to show), and he bided his time until the day when he would have the power to fight bigotry.

LOW MARKS, DIVORCE, AND VIETNAM

Steven's problems with anti-Semites weren't helped by the fact that he didn't like school. He didn't pay attention in class, and his grades went down. In *E.T.*, the lead character asks, "How do you explain school to higher intelligence?" This question might have been on Steven's mind during his not-so-great experience in school. His parents hired tutors for him, but it didn't help. He barely managed to graduate from high school with a low C average.

During this period, Arnold and Leah's marriage was failing. Night after night, Steven and his sisters heard their parents arguing in their bedroom. The raised voices and bitter tones made Steven wonder if he, the eldest, shared the responsibility for the unhappiness that was tearing his family apart.

Finally, in 1965, the year Steven graduated from high school, his parents separated and then divorced. On the heels of the divorce and his graduation, Steven had to face the fact that many of the better colleges would not accept him as a student because of his poor grades. And not going to college meant that he could be drafted into the armed services.

Being sent to Vietnam was a concern of many young men during the mid-1960s. "I would have done anything to stay out of Vietnam," says Spielberg. Barred by his low grade-point average from attending a major film school, he managed to get into California State College in Long Beach. It had no film school, but he

> **"I would have done anything to stay out of Vietnam."**

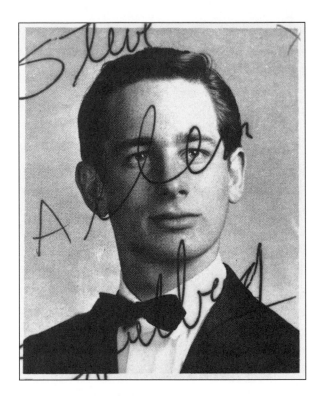

Steven autographed this 1965 senior photo for his high school yearbook. His middle name was misspelled, so he signed the photo to match the yearbook spelling.

majored in English. As a college student, he was exempt from the military.

CHASING A MOVIE CAREER

Spielberg attended California State College for three years. During much of that time he paid very little attention to his classes. He arranged his schedule so that he only had to be in class two days a week. The rest of the week was devoted to movies. Ever since junior high school, he had known that the only career he could possibly pursue was that of a film director.

He spent much of his time watching foreign films in Los Angeles. He studied the techniques of European directors, such as Luis Buñuel, Vittorio De Sica, and Ingmar Bergman. "I must have seen every Bergman movie ever made," he recalls. Sometimes he worked in the college cafeteria to scrape up the money to buy film to make short features using the techniques he studied. Often, he altered those techniques. He was finding his own voice as a director.

Around this time, Steven took a guided tour of Universal Studios. On purpose, he lagged behind the tour group in order to roam around the movie lot on his own. He sneaked onto a sound stage where a TV film was being shot. He wandered into an editing room and talked to some film editors. They spoke his language. When he told them he'd made some movies, they told him to bring them in so they could take a look at them. He was back the next day with *Firelight* and some other 8-mm films he had shot.

After that day, Spielberg put on a suit and tie, bluffed his way past the guard at the gate, and hung out at Universal three or four days a week for months. He did volunteer office work for the studio, and he wandered from department to department, asking questions, storing away information, and learning his craft.

STARTING HIS CAREER

Spielberg realized that if he wanted to crash the film business, he would have to make a movie more professional than *Firelight*. Then he'd have to get a **studio** executive to look at his work. That opportunity required money. He scraped up some of it from his parents and other relatives. But what really made his first big project possible was the $20,000 invested by a Hollywood businessman, Denis C. Hoffman. That $20,000 enabled Spielberg to make the movie he would call *Amblin'*.

Although *Amblin'* ran only twenty-four minutes, it took a year to shoot. The storyline is simple. Two young people meet in the Mojave Desert. They hitchhike to the California coast together, and they become lovers. There is one very brief love scene and not very much else in the way of plot. Mood, scenery, lighting, and action were all designed to show how well Steven had learned the tricks of directing.

The short movie won an award at the Atlanta Film Festival in 1969. Spielberg's film came to the attention of Sidney J. Sheinberg, a Universal executive. "I thought it was terrific," Sheinberg later told an interviewer. He asked to see Spielberg.

A WORLD OF MAKE-BELIEVE

Very nervously, Spielberg responded to the call from Sheinberg. He was afraid that his unauthorized presence on the Universal lot had been discovered. Instead, he was dumbfounded to hear Sheinberg saying how much he liked *Amblin'*. He was even more bowled over when Sheinberg offered him a contract to direct films for television.

"But I have a year left to go in college," Steven blurted out.

"Do you want to go to college, or do you want to direct?" Sheinberg inquired.

Spielberg didn't have to think about his answer. He recalls, "I left [school] so quickly that I never even cleaned out my locker." A few weeks later, he signed a seven-year contract with Universal. "My father will never forgive me for leaving college," Spielberg sighs. Nevertheless, his new job at Universal was the fulfillment of a dream.

CHAPTER FOUR

BUILDING A CAREER

Spielberg's first assignment was a TV drama segment starring 62-year-old Academy Award-winning actress Joan Crawford. Spielberg "heard later that she had been promised a [top] director, like George Cukor, and had no idea that they were going to assign an acne-ridden, sniffling-nosed, first-time-out director." Crawford protested. She said to the newcomer, "People will think you're my son, not my director." Still, the studio refused to take Spielberg off the picture.

STUCK WITH EACH OTHER

The film was to be one-third of a **pilot** for a new TV series called "Night Gallery." The pilot, which was meant to spin off the success of Rod Serling's popular "Twilight Zone" series, consisted of three stories written and presented by Serling. In 1969, Spielberg directed the middle story, entitled "Eyes."

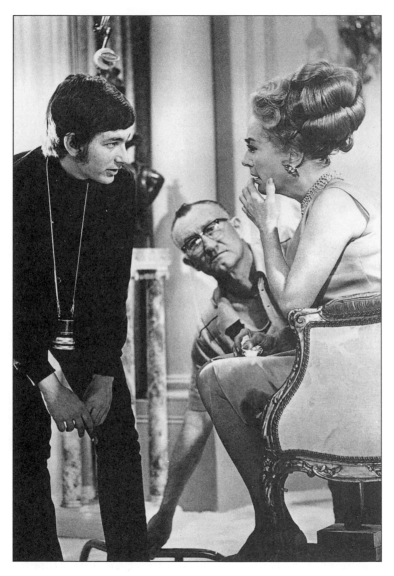

*In 1969, Spielberg directs Joan Crawford
on the set of "Eyes."*

Crawford was being paid an impressive $50,000 to star in this film about a wealthy, blind woman who is desperate to see again. (Spielberg was taking home less than $100 a week after taxes at this time.)

Spielberg's first reaction when he read the script was to try to get out of directing the movie. However, he was no more successful in avoiding the assignment than Crawford had been in trying to have him fired. They were stuck with each other.

CONFLICT AND COMPROMISE

"I couldn't wait to get off the picture," Spielberg remembers. All the same, he tried to placate Crawford. Her late husband was the president of Pepsi-Cola, so each day Spielberg made a ceremony out of presenting her with a Pepsi-Cola bottle with a rose in it. She would drink down the bottle, burp, and then drive him crazy with her complaints and demands.

"I couldn't wait to get off the picture."

Crawford couldn't remember her lines, and Spielberg had to print up giant-size **cue cards** that she could read through the bandages her character wore after an eye operation. She constantly asked him to define her character's actions and reactions. Spielberg couldn't do that because he hadn't written the script—and he wasn't too happy with the character himself. She challenged his decisions at every turn. When she demanded **retakes,** he gave in to her.

Despite the friction, when the film was completed, Crawford presented Spielberg with a bottle of cologne and a man's bracelet. The studio later informed Spielberg that they weren't happy with the segment and were "going to have to perform major surgery on your show." Spielberg was so discouraged that he announced he was quitting. However, Sidney J. Sheinberg persuaded him to take a leave of absence without pay instead.

THE TELEVISION YEARS

After four months, Spielberg returned to Universal. The word was out that his first directing assignment, "Eyes," had required extensive revisions, and now nobody wanted to work with him. Finally, he was assigned to the doctor drama, "Marcus Welby, M.D.," and he directed six installments of the TV series. They did little to enhance his reputation, though.

Over the next two years, assignments for other series followed. Spielberg directed episodes for "The Psychiatrists," "The Name of the Game," "Owen Marshall," and "Columbo," but he saw no future in such assignments. What he really wanted was to direct a full-length movie. He recognized that Universal was not going to assign him to direct a movie for distribution to theaters. The best he could hope for was a feature-length movie for television. By chance, he read a short story called "Duel," by Richard Matheson, in a magazine. The story had just the potential for the visual suspense and heart-pounding action Spielberg was seeking.

DIRECTING *DUEL*

Duel was about a businessman making a car trip. He becomes involved in a car chase with a truck driver. The suspense builds as the truck and car zoom around the curving roads and hairpin turns of the mountains. Finally they crash and both vehicles hurtle into a quarry. The trucker is killed, but the hero survives.

Universal viewed *Duel* as a possible TV Movie of the Week. The studio assigned the lead to Dennis Weaver, the star of "McCloud," a popular TV series.

Taking his lead from renowned suspense director Alfred Hitchcock, Spielberg laid out the film in **storyboards.** Stick figures nailed down the poses and positioning for the actors. It was like a giant comic book. One of Spielberg's storyboards for *Duel* was 40 yards (37 meters) long!

Spielberg took only sixteen days to shoot *Duel*. It ran two-and-a-half hours, much too long for television. Spielberg painstakingly cut it to one hour and fifteen minutes. It was first broadcast on November 13, 1971.

Viewers and critics alike heaped praise on *Duel*. It became popular among people in the television and film industry. The film's fame was spread by word of mouth long after the initial showing. In 1973, *Duel* was distributed for theater viewing in Europe, as well as Japan and Australia. It won film festival awards in Italy, West Germany, and Monaco. *Duel* eventually earned $6 million.

THE SUGARLAND EXPRESS

Spielberg correctly saw the success of *Duel* as his ticket to directing big-screen movies. When a story in the *Los Angeles Citizen News* caught his attention, he clipped it. It was about a 1969 incident in Texas. A convicted shoplifter had been trying to get her two-year-old child out of foster care after she was released from prison. She helped her husband break out of jail, and they kidnapped a state trooper. Spielberg enlisted **screenwriters** Hal Barwood and Matthew Robbins to develop a script based on the clipping.

Universal agreed to let Spielberg make the film. It would be called *The Sugarland Express*. The studio had signed the star of the TV comedy *Laugh-In*—Goldie Hawn. She had won a Best Supporting Actress Oscar for *Cactus Flower*, and Spielberg was happy with the casting.

Sugarland Express was shot on location in Texas. Shooting began on January 15, 1973. The plot, which had many comic incidents, was constructed to end in tragedy. Spielberg had decided to shoot it in a way that would build suspense and lead up to an impressive, action-filled climax.

THE SPIELBERG TOUCH

In the movie, Goldie Hawn and her screen husband, William Atherton, kidnap a lawman and force him to drive them across Texas in his police car. Soon they are being pursued in a 150-mile (about 241-kilometer) chase by some ninety police cars. As more cars join the chase, a bumper-to-bumper situation is created. To film the spectacle, Spielberg used a newly invented Panaflex 35-mm camera. This allowed him to create 360-degree **panning shots** of the chase.

Doubtful about Spielberg, Richard Zanuck, one of the two producers Universal had assigned to oversee the film, had gone on location to observe the shooting of the tricky scene. Zanuck recalls, "Here he was, a young little punk kid, with a lot of seasoned crew around, a major actress on hand, and instead of starting with something easy, he picked a very complicated thing that required all sorts of intricate timing."

Nevertheless, Zanuck concluded, "It worked incredibly well." This distinctive, sweeping pho-

Spielberg in 1973, during the time he was directing
The Sugarland Express

tography of fast-paced scenes would later become
a hallmark of the Spielberg style. When *Sugarland* was released, film professionals were very
impressed with the young director's style.

  Sugarland Express, however, was not a big
moneymaker. Spielberg was regarded in the business as a highly talented young director who
might not be able to attract the large audiences
needed to make a profit at the box office. But that
opinion was about to change forever. A very special fish was waiting to be immortalized by
Spielberg.

CHAPTER FIVE

THE GREAT WHITE SHARK

One weekend in 1974, producers at Universal gave Spielberg a soon-to-be-published novel—*Jaws*. After reading it, Spielberg recognized that it had the potential to both alarm and entertain audiences, just as he knew what would frighten and delight his sisters when he was younger. The following Monday morning, Spielberg walked into the producers' offices and said, "Let me direct this film." He got his wish, but Spielberg accepted the job on one condition: in order to build the audience's terror about the man-eating shark, he did not want to show the shark for the first hour of the film.

"Let me direct this film."

Spielberg opens *Jaws* with a scene of an attractive young woman swimming in a calm ocean. The camera follows her as she swims underwater and picks up a shadow. It looms larger and larger. Suddenly, there is a violent thrashing in the water, and a struggle follows. But the audience does not see much of what is happening. Spielberg leaves the horror to the viewer's imagination. The suspense and expectation—not what people see, but what they expect to see—keeps viewers on the edge of their seats.

The very sight of movement in the water—sunlight striking the tailfin of a fish or a child moving seaward in the surf—is enough to make audiences squeal with anticipated horror. By the time the dread shark actually leaps into view, some feel it is a disappointment. According to the *New York Times* review of the film, it is "nothing more than a creaky, old-fashioned monster."

IF YOU BUILD IT, THEY WILL COME

One of Spielberg's big problems with *Jaws* was the shark. Despite his efforts to shoot footage of great white sharks, his endeavor was largely a failure. If he couldn't film a real shark, Spielberg decided he would have to build a mechanical one. Twenty years earlier, Bob Mattey had made his reputation by creating the giant squid that attacked the submarine in *20,000 Leagues Under the Sea*. Now, intrigued by the problems creating a great white shark presented, Mattey agreed to to build Spielberg's oceanic monster.

Mattey nicknamed the shark Bruce. He devised an underwater sled to move it around. Resting on the sled was a 12-foot (3.6-m) movable steel tower. Constructed of steel and polyurethane, Bruce sat atop the tower attached to controls that moved its jaws and fins and made it leap.

Actually, three Bruces were built, and all three had problems. Sometimes, when the sled was towed across the ocean bottom, the shark moved jerkily and unrealistically through the water. When it surfaced, there were times when its eyes crossed. In addition, its bloody jaws refused to close on its make-believe prey. Each of the three Bruces weighed one and a half tons and cost $150,000 to build. The high salaries of the technicians who ran the mechanical sharks doubled the costs. One Bruce sank like a rock. Another exploded.

These glitches made Spielberg frantic. He was fighting a tight schedule and running over budget. Mattey worked to fix the problems, but he refused to be hurried. "Ask him what time it is," Spielberg gritted his teeth, "and he'll tell you how to build a watch."

SINKING THE ORCA

Other problems ran up the costs and slowed down the production. The location for shooting the film proved problematic. Spielberg had selected the village of Edgartown, on the island of Martha's

Vineyard off Cape Cod, Massachusetts. He thought the deep water offshore and the typical tides of only three feet (ninety centimeters) would make shooting relatively easy. He was wrong. The tides proved to be unpredictable. Storms caused costly delays in shooting the action sequences with the shark.

The worst mishap involved the *Orca*, the ship on which actors Richard Dreyfuss, Roy Scheider, and Robert Shaw set out to destroy the shark. The plot climax called for the *Orca* to be attacked and sunk by the shark. Underwater cables were supposed to drag the boat down, demonstrating the strength of the shark.

While the boat was being dragged, Spielberg was shooting Scheider in the cabin of the *Orca*. Suddenly a large chunk of the boat ripped loose. Spielberg and Scheider went flying. Two cameras were lost over the side, along with a large amount of film footage. The footage was irreplaceable, but luck was with Spielberg. The film was rescued from the water, and it was restorable.

ACTORS V. DIRECTOR

Throughout the filming of *Jaws*, Spielberg had problems with his actors. He caused some of the conflicts because of the way he treated them. Spielberg distanced himself from cast and crew. Some saw him as petulant, complaining that

Spielberg (center, right) relaxes aboard the Orca *with Robert Shaw (left), Roy Scheider (center, left), and Richard Dreyfuss (right).*

when he was displeased, he retreated into stony silences. To be fair, though, the lead actors caused some of the difficulties.

The three main roles in *Jaws* are relatively equal, and competition among Dreyfuss, Shaw, and Scheider was inevitable. The most experienced actor, Shaw—who played the feisty professional shark hunter—took one look at the relatively inexperienced Dreyfuss and Scheider and decided he could steal the film from them. In the opinion of many critics, he succeeded.

Spielberg recognized what Shaw was doing, and there were tense moments between them. His relationship with Dreyfuss was even stormier. Dreyfuss, with only two movies behind him, already had a reputation for being "hard to handle." As technical difficulties held up shooting on *Jaws*, the actor became convinced that the picture was going to be a disaster and would ruin his career.

BECOMING A MILLIONAIRE

As problems piled up, the cost of shooting *Jaws* mounted. The time it took Spielberg to persuade Universal to let him go overbudget cut into his concentration on the film. Originally, *Jaws* had been budgeted at $3.5 million. In the end, it cost $9.8 million to make.

Jaws opened on June 20, 1975. Afraid it might flop, the studio took steps to prevent negative reviews and word of mouth from building. The film had its initial showings in only 407 theaters in the United States and 55 in Canada. Spielberg, also nervous about its reception, agreed with this decision.

The reviews were mixed. There were many

raves, but some reviews belittled *Jaws* as a movie made solely for money. Those critics did not convince audiences to avoid the film, however. *Jaws* took in an incredible $60 million at the box office during the first month of its release. Eventually it grossed $260 million in the United States alone. It surpassed *The Godfather* as the highest-grossing film up to that time. Spielberg received $3 million as his share of the film's earnings. Now Hollywood's youngest director was a millionaire.

To that accomplishment, he added the distinction of inventing the idea of a summer blockbuster. Before *Jaws*, film studios did not release movies that were expected to make much money in the summer. After Spielberg's phenomenal success with *Jaws*, studios began producing popcorn movies, many with special effects, geared to attracting ticket-buyers during summer vacation. Since *Jaws*, each summer has seen a bombardment of these summer blockbusters, such as *Independence Day* (1998) and *Star Wars: The Phantom Menace* (1999).

CHAPTER SIX

THE HEARTBREAK KID

In 1976, on the heels of his success with *Jaws*, Spielberg met a young actress, Amy Irving, at a charity premiere. Her effect on him was electric. The workaholic director fell in love.

Before that night, he had dated only casually. Lacking in social skills and not caring that he did, Spielberg avoided the Hollywood party scene. He was awkward with women, and his focus was on his career. But Irving changed that. She was different.

That first night they had talked easily, and he'd been comfortable with her. Besides, she was beautiful. Radiant and slender, with attentive green eyes and a waterfall of chestnut hair, she could have had her pick of handsome men in Hollywood. He was flattered that she was attracted to him.

REMAKING OF THE NERD

Irving liked to ski. She flew a sailplane. She was an outspoken, ambitious young woman at the beginning of a promising acting career. It took Spielberg a month to get up the courage to call Irving after their first meeting. To his joy, he found that his very quirkiness and intelligence and cinema know-how drew her to him. She didn't care that he was awkward and not as athletic as she was. They became lovers.

The relationship changed Spielberg. He came out of his shell. He began to enjoy socializing, taking pleasure in entering a roomful of people with the lovely Irving on his arm. He took an interest in art. He grew a beard. Under her guidance, he began to dress more stylishly, even wearing a suit and necktie now and then.

FRIENDLY EXTRATERRESTRIALS

At the time Spielberg met Irving, he was already hard at work on a **screenplay** for his next movie. There had been many films dealing with aliens from outer space who were bent on conquering or destroying Earth. Spielberg, however, had long held a different view of extraterrestrial life. He realized that "in thirty years of UFO reportings, the encounters have been very benevolent. No sci-fi death rays, no radiation poisoning." Now he wanted to make a movie about aliens who might frighten earthlings, but who would turn out to be friendly. He was also inspired by the experience of seeing a meteor shower with his father.

The film would be called *Close Encounters of the Third Kind*. Among those who study UFO evidence, sightings are encounters of the first kind. Physical evidence of alien presence on Earth is an encounter of the second kind. Actual contact with extraterrestrials marks the third kind of encounter.

Spielberg did extensive research. He interviewed pilots, astronomers, NASA technicians, and scientists. As a consultant on the film, he hired J. Allen Hynek, who coined the term "close encounter" in his book, *The UFO Experience*.

CASTING CALL

After *Jaws*, Spielberg and Universal had parted company. He brought his new project to Columbia Pictures, and they agreed to finance it with a budget of $8 million. Spielberg hired Douglas Trumbull to do the special effects. Having done the special effects for *Star Wars* (1977) and *2001: A Space Odyssey* (1968), Trumbull was considered the best in the business.

Despite his problems with Richard Dreyfuss on *Jaws*, Spielberg wanted him to play the lead in

Close Encounters. Dreyfuss was reluctant. He wanted more money than Spielberg was offering. However, when he heard that Gene Hackman, Al Pacino, and Jack Nicholson were all being considered for the part, he agreed to the deal.

Casting the other leads was easier. Teri Garr, Melinda Dillon, four-year-old Cary Guffey and French film director François Truffaut readily agreed to play the roles Steven had written for them. The next problem was harder to solve—where to shoot a film with such spacious demands.

Spielberg and Trumbull finally settled on four locations: the Mojave Desert; Bombay, India; Gillette, Wyoming; and a former Air Force base in Mobile, Alabama. There were four huge hangars on the base. One of them became the largest **sound stage** in the history of movies. It was six times as large as the average sound stage.

CLOSE ENCOUNTERS OF THE THIRD KIND

Tight security barred the media from the Alabama complex. Spielberg didn't want the movie to be bad-mouthed before its release as *Jaws* had been. Since the special effects were going to be added later, the actors often didn't know what was going on during a particular scene. Spielberg didn't want them guessing in earshot of the media.

He was getting along better with his actors now than he did on *Jaws*. He was somewhat intimidated by having the legendary director Truffaut involved. He said, "Directing a movie with Truffaut on the set is like having Renoir around when you're still painting by numbers." Nevertheless, Spielberg was thrilled to work with someone as renowned as Truffaut. Writing to friends in Paris, Truffaut described Spielberg as "unpretentious, good-humored, and patient, with an enthusiasm that was infectious." His more relaxed attitude doubtless sprang from the regular visits of Amy Irving to Mobile. Steven basked in her presence.

"Directing a movie with Truffaut on the set is like having Renoir around when you're still painting by numbers."

It took five months to shoot *Close Encounters* and another year of painstaking work to edit it. By then, the original budget had grown from $8 million to $18 million. Before the movie was released, the media said that it was a colossal flop. *Close Encounters of the Third Kind* opened at the Ziegfeld Theater in New York City on November 15, 1977. The preview was a great success. The audience gave the film a standing ovation. With only a few exceptions, the reviews were positive, and many critics were wild about the film. Back in Hollywood, Steven Spielberg was hailed as a genius.

THE KAMIKAZE COMEDY

Spielberg now had directed two back-to-back smash hits. In 1976, *Jaws* had received an Oscar nomination for Best Picture, and he received another one in 1978 for directing *Close Encounters*. (He did not win either award.) He was in love with a beautiful woman who loved him. His contemporaries heaped praise on him. He had it all. What more could any man want?

Another hit movie, that's what. Even as he was editing *Close Encounters,* Spielberg was lining up his next project. It was to be his first comedy, set in World War II right after the attack on Pearl Harbor and appropriately titled *1941*.

The picture was top-heavy with talent—featuring megastars Dan Aykroyd and John Belushi—before it even started shooting. Sadly, the script overwhelmed the actors. The special effects, formerly Spielberg's strong point, now proved his undoing. The climax was overshadowed by the destruction of an amusement park, in which a Ferris wheel rolls down seaside cliffs into the ocean. By the time that point was reached, audiences had lost track of the many diversions from the main plot. Reviewers heaped scorn on *1941*. Critic Pauline Kael said that sitting through it was like "having your head inside a pinball machine for two hours." Audiences stayed away.

THE BREAKUP

The failure shook up Spielberg. Irving was supportive, but then she went on location in Texas for her role in *Honeysuckle Rose*. Before she left, she and Spielberg discussed going to Japan, getting married there, and staying for a three-week honeymoon. Irving confided in friends, "We can't wait to start a family."

In *Honeysuckle Rose*, Irving played a young folk singer who goes on tour with a married country and western superstar twice her age. The male role fit real-life country singer Willie Nelson like a glove. He was gnarled and aging, but his charisma leaped out at audiences from the screen just as it did in live concerts. In the film, Irving's character and Nelson's have a torrid love affair. As it turned out, Irving wasn't immune to Nelson's charisma off the screen either. Their affair was a case of real life copying art. Nevertheless, when filming was completed, Irving returned to California and Spielberg.

They left for Japan in December 1979. Only Irving and Spielberg know if she told him about her affair with Nelson on that flight, or if something else happened between them to change their plans. What is known is that Spielberg returned to Los Angeles alone.

Their breakup devastated him. He told

friends that Irving's rejection had hurt him even worse than his parents' divorce. He said, "I suffer like I'm sixteen. It's a miracle I haven't sprouted acne again."

"I suffer like I'm sixteen. It's a miracle I haven't sprouted acne again."

After the failure of *1941*, it was whispered that his talent was waning and he was on the skids. Spielberg was over the age of thirty by now. It pained him when a journalist referred to him as "a wastrel, a man who had seen his best days before he was thirty."

CHAPTER SEVEN

George Lucas, the writer-director of the smash-hit movie *Star Wars*, played a major role in reviving Spielberg's career as a director. The two had known each other since the days when they were both trying to break into films. In the late 1970s, they had a conversation about how much they had enjoyed the Saturday matinee chapter serials at the movies as kids. They thought it would be fun to do a feature-length film structured like those cliffhangers.

CASTING INDIANA JONES

Lucas had written a story for the cliffhanger project they'd discussed and assigned writer Lawrence Kasdan to do a screenplay. The movie based on Kasdan's screenplay was *Raiders of the Lost Ark*. Lucasfilm produced it. From the first,

Spielberg with George Lucas. Both men began their careers as directors in the 1960s.

Lucas was certain that only one man could direct *Raiders*—Spielberg.

In *Raiders,* the hero is Indiana Jones, a daring archaeologist who is first seen searching for treasure in the South American jungle. In the course of the film, he confronts and overcomes torturing Nazis, sword-wielding giants, poisonous snakes, even more poisonous spiders, angry natives, and rockslides. Spielberg's first problem was to find an actor who could live up to the character as written.

He interviewed Harrison Ford, who had been one of the leads in *Star Wars*. Ford loved the character and wanted the role. Meanwhile, however, Spielberg had second thoughts and decided that the more powerfully built Tom Selleck should play the part. Ford was furious. However, CBS picked up an option on Selleck's services for the TV series "Magnum, P. I.," and he was no longer available. Spielberg went back to Ford. He accepted the role, but he never quite got over his anger at being second choice.

CAST COMPLICATIONS

Originally, Spielberg had thought of Amy Irving for the film's female lead, but after their painful breakup, that idea was no longer possible. He cast Karen Allen, a relative newcomer. He hired mostly English and European actors for the rest of the cast. One actor described the plot of the film as "the Bible with Nazis."

Raiders was shot on location in England, France, Nepal, Hawaii, and Tunisia. During the filming of *Raiders,* Spielberg was very hard on his actors and his crew. Lucas had given him seventy-three days to shoot the picture, and cracking the whip was the only way Spielberg knew of staying within such a tight schedule. "Sometimes I was the only person on the set who was talking to

Spielberg (left) discusses a scene with Karen Allen (center) and Harrison Ford (right) during the filming of Raiders of the Lost Ark.

him," remembers British actor Paul Freeman. Another English cast member, Alfred Molina, threatened to quit when Spielberg ordered his bare back covered with large, hairy tarantulas. Harrison Ford and Karen Allen balked at the prospect of dealing with 4,500 snakes—boa constrictors and cobras—even though glass separated them from the reptiles. Given his childhood nightmares of snakes, Spielberg probably did not blame Ford and Allen for being wary. Finally, anti-venom was flown in from India, and an ambulance stood by throughout the shooting with the snakes. As it turned out, the anti-venom was so old that it had lost its potency and would have been of no help in case of snakebite. Fortunately, it never had to be put to the test.

SPIELBERG SCORES AGAIN

In the summer of 1981, *Raiders of the Lost Ark* was completed and released to theaters. Spielberg loved the film. He said, "The film's like popcorn. It doesn't fill you up. It's easy to digest. And it melts in your mouth. It's the kind of thing you can just go back and chow down over and over again. . . . I love making movies like that." Some critics brushed it off as childish while others, such as Pauline Kael of *The New Yorker,* thought it lacked "exhilaration." Such criticisms didn't matter. Audiences—children and adults alike—loved it. *Raiders* was the big hit of the summer. In its first year of release, it earned $310 million. It was another smash hit for Steven Spielberg.

> "The film's like popcorn. It doesn't fill you up. It's easy to digest. And it melts in your mouth."

CHAPTER EIGHT

E.T. THE EXTRA-TERRESTRIAL

In 1982, one year after *Raiders of the Lost Ark* was released, the film *Poltergeist* debuted. Spielberg was co-producer and had also contributed to the story for the script. The film was a scary ghost story, and it had moviegoers screaming aloud. Spielberg told interviewers that it was "all about the terrible things I did to my younger sisters during my childhood."

Meanwhile, he had once again been nominated for an Oscar for his directing of *Raiders of the Lost Ark*. The film had also received a nomination for Best Picture. Neither Spielberg nor *Raiders* received an Oscar in 1982. It seemed that the Hollywood establishment was never going to take him seriously.

AN IDEA TAKES SHAPE

When word leaked out about his next project, it did nothing to dispel the view that Spielberg was

▲ 62 ▲

a lightweight. The project had begun with an idea that had been rattling around in Spielberg's head since he was a child. The story was about a lonely boy who becomes friends with a visitor from another planet. Spielberg had always seen the story as a sort of buddy movie in which the visitor and the boy establish a relationship based on their mutual alienation from the suburban world around them.

Spielberg identified with the boy, remembering his own boyhood isolation. He said, "*E.T.* was a movie about my childhood—about my parents' divorce, although people haven't often seen that it's about divorce. "[When] my parents split up . . . I needed a special friend and had to use my imagination to take me to places

"[When] my parents split up . . . I needed a special friend and had to use my imagination to take me to places that felt good."

that felt good—that helped me move beyond the problems my parents were having, and that ended our family as a whole. And thinking about that time, I thought, an extraterrestrial character would be the perfect springboard to purge the pain of your parents' splitting up." He described *E.T.* as "the closest film to my own sensibilities, my own fantasies, my own heart."

One night, he casually told his idea to a

screenwriter friend, Melissa Mathison. It touched her deeply, and she told Spielberg that he simply had to make the film. Her fervent response persuaded him to ask her to try writing a screenplay.

Mathison eventually conceived E.T. as a 900-year-old extraterrestrial, a botanist stranded in a world that is completely strange to him. In a typical American suburb, ten-year-old Elliott discovers E.T. The bond between Elliott and E.T. goes beyond empathy to actually experiencing each other's emotional and physical feelings: when E.T. drinks beer, Elliott gets drunk; when Elliott is instructed to kill a frog in biology class, E.T.'s revulsion is so strong that Elliott frees all the frogs in the school laboratory; when Elliott kisses a little girl, E.T. is thrilled.

CREATING AN ALIEN FROM OUTER SPACE

Although the connection between E.T. and Elliott is charming, the visual imagery and the feelings *E.T.* generates make the film the classic it is. The look of the movie and the sense of wonder it creates turn adult viewers into wide-eyed children. Most of all, it is E.T. who steals scene after scene from a trio of excellent child actors to win the hearts of audiences. The bug-eyed monster with the frog-like voice was the most endearing creature to take over the screen since Lassie the collie.

Spielberg hired Carlo Rambaldi, who had worked on *Close Encounters,* to create E.T. Spielberg pasted together a collage to show Rambaldi what he wanted the face to convey. He used a baby's face, poet Carl Sandburg's eyes, the forehead of Ernest Hemingway, and the nose of Albert Einstein. The result was a combination of infant innocence and elderly experience encased in a skull shaped like a hammer and a face crisscrossed with wrinkles of worried wisdom.

Spielberg directs Henry Thomas,
who played Elliot in E.T.

Mathison had wanted the body of E.T. to be more vegetable-like than animal. Rambaldi compromised, adding an inner green light that lit up like a pulsing heart when E.T. was displaying emotion. Spielberg used recordings of otter calls as E.T.'s outer-space gibberish. When actual speech from the alien was called for, actress Debra Winger's croaking voice was dubbed in.

ON THE HORIZON

E.T. the Extra-Terrestrial opened on June 11, 1982 to rave reviews. *E.T.* was the kind of movie that many people, particularly children, went back to see two and three times. The film received several Academy Award nominations, including Best Picture, Best Director, and Original Screenplay. In March 1983, however, it did not receive awards in these major categories, illustrating that the distance between Spielberg's movies and the taste of Academy voters had not narrowed. *E.T.* did win four technical Oscars—for Scoring, Sound, Sound Effects Editing, and Visual Effects.

Nevertheless, most people agreed that *E.T.* was the year's best entertainment. Some people said it was the best film of the decade, and some equated *E.T.* to *The Wizard of Oz*. It was certainly a happy time for Spielberg, and the success of *E.T.* was not the only reason that life was good for him.

Spielberg and E.T.

There was a new love in Spielberg's life, as well as an old love about to be rediscovered. Happiness and heartbreak were both on the horizon.

CHAPTER NINE

THE COLOR PURPLE

Following *E.T.*, Spielberg became involved in two film projects. One was *Twilight Zone: The Movie.* The other was *Indiana Jones and the Temple of Doom,* a sequel to *Raiders of the Lost Ark.* He was **executive producer** of both and directed one of the four segments in *Twilight Zone* as well as the *Indiana Jones* film.

Harrison Ford starred in the sequel. Kate Capshaw, a young actress who had made her mark in soap operas, played opposite him. Originally from Texas, Capshaw was a divorcée with a daughter and a master's degree in learning disabilities. Behind her quick laugh and vivacious personality, there was a keen intelligence. Soon, the director and his star were romantically involved.

A CHANCE MEETING

Spielberg, Capshaw, the cast, and crew arrived in India to shoot scenes for *Temple of*

Doom. There, Steven bumped into Amy Irving, who was filming another movie. Their chance meeting led to dinner, and soon Spielberg was spending all his spare time with Irving. Now he saw Capshaw only on the set, where he was directing her. Spielberg's relationship with Irving deepened throughout the shooting of *Temple of Doom.* The film was released in 1984 amid strong protests from parents and critics. They complained that it was too violent for children. Some demanded that *Temple of Doom* be given an X rating—the equivalent of today's NC-17 rating. The complaints were resolved when a PG-13 rating—suggesting parental guidance for children under the age of thirteen—was devised by the Motion Picture Association of America.

A DIFFERENT KIND OF MOVIE

As always, controversy did not slow down Spielberg. While he was preparing another major directing project, he was functioning as executive producer on four other films. They were *Gremlins, The Goonies* (for which he also wrote the story), *Young Sherlock Holmes,* and *Back to the Future.*

He realized that he had fallen into a pattern of making the same type of film. Spielberg said, "After *E.T.,* people expected a certain kind of film from me, a certain amount of screams and cheers and laughs and thrills. And I was caving in to that. I knew I could give it to them, but I realize it made me a little arrogant about my own style. It was all too easy. The whole titillation I've always felt about the unknown—of seeing that tree outside my bedroom window and shutting the drapes till morning—was taken away from me. And I got scared. I don't want to see where I'm going."

The Color Purple was very different from anything Spielberg had ever directed before. The book, by Alice Walker, had won the Pulitzer Prize for Fiction and the American Book Award. But *The Color Purple* was not an adventure story. There were no cliffhanger sequences. There were no aliens from outer space. There were no opportunities for special effects or high-tech monsters. And it was not a tale for children. The movie was about race and poverty, rape and incest. By Hollywood standards, this was not a typical Spielberg movie. Nevertheless, he was determined to make it. He explained, "I wanted to do this book because I was scared I couldn't."

> **"I wanted to do this book because I was scared I couldn't."**

THE WRONG DIRECTOR?

From the first, there was controversy about Spielberg directing *The Color Purple*. Some activists

In 1985, Spielberg gives suggestions to Whoopi Goldberg during the filming of The Color Purple.

wanted an African-American director. Women's groups worried that his films lacked sensitivity to the female concerns central to *The Color Purple*. Lesbian spokespersons questioned how he would deal with the same-sex relationship in the book.

Walker had faith that Spielberg would remain true to her work, however. Her one condition, she told Spielberg, was that "the final cast, though not stars or widely known, must seem like they have stepped straight from the book." She passed along to Spielberg a letter from a stand-up comic who wanted to play Sofia in *The Color Purple*.

The comic's name was Whoopi Goldberg. Walker recommended her to Spielberg for the main part of Celie, which Goldberg eventually played. Given her inexperience as a serious actress, many thought it an example of serious miscasting. There were also misgivings about casting talk-show host Oprah Winfrey and little-known Margaret Avery in the other main female parts. However, Spielberg cast recognized actors Danny Glover and Adolph Caesar in the main male roles.

FATHERHOOD AND MARRIAGE

Dealing with the real world and the hardships and feelings of real people was a new experience for Spielberg. It required him to be in touch with his own feelings in a way that he had never allowed himself to be before. Spielberg said, "The idea of separation—families torn apart, the feeling of unrequited love, and feeling like a stranger in a land that was supposedly made for you and me—I thought those were subjects I could speak honestly about." He admits that when he read the book, he "cried and cried at the end." He wanted to convey the emotions of Walker's book and those he had been feeling as he immersed himself in making the movie.

Spielberg was going through an emotional period while he was directing *The Color Purple*. While he'd been casting, Irving had informed him that he was going to be a father. In June 1985, just as he was filming the scene in which the main character gives birth, he received word that Irving was in labor.

> "The idea of separation—families torn apart, the feeling of unrequited love, and feeling like a stranger in a land that was supposedly made for you and me—I thought those were subjects I could speak honestly about."

On June 13, a son, Max Samuel, was born. Spielberg was present at the birth, and he cut Max's umbilical cord.

On November 27, 1985, Spielberg and Irving were married. They were on their honeymoon in Paris when *The Color Purple* opened. They didn't read the reviews.

ALWAYS A BRIDESMAID

The film ran 152 minutes. The critics thought it was too long and lacked unity. They said that where the book had been a blistering attack on inhumanity and racism, the movie was a sugar-substitute, hearts-and-flowers version of that theme. Some African-American groups picketed the theaters where *The Color Purple* was playing, claiming it stereotyped black men as brutal and lied about the poverty of blacks in the South. Lesbian groups protested Spielberg's blurring the same-sex experiences that had been spelled out in the book.

Audiences, however, flocked to see the movie. From all reports, they liked it. Many felt that *The Color Purple* communicated deep emotions that mainstream movies had been neglecting for some time. The movie earned more than $140 million at the box office. Along with the film's popular success came Academy Award recognition. *The Color Purple* received a nomination for Best Picture. Whoopi Goldberg was nominated for Best Actress and Oprah Winfrey and Margaret Avery both received nominations for Best Supporting Actress. Spielberg was not nominated for Best Director. No one associated with *The Color Purple* won any Oscars in 1986. In protest, the Directors Guild of America named Spielberg Best Director. It seemed that Spielberg was destined to make profitable films without honor from the Academy.

CHAPTER TEN

DIVORCE AND DINOSAURS

Following *The Color Purple,* Spielberg functioned as a producer on five films before directing his next picture, *Empire of the Sun.* During this period, he was as deeply involved at home as he was on the job. His main focus was his wife and their son.

He was more relaxed and free of the tension that usually built up when he was directing. Hollywood finally chose to recognize him. At the Academy Award ceremony in 1987, Spielberg received the Irving Thalberg Memorial Award, honoring the high quality of his work as a producer.

EMPIRE OF THE SUN

Also in 1987, after long negotiations with the Chinese government for permission to shoot in Shanghai, Spielberg went back to directing.

Spielberg, Amy Irving, and their son, Max, in 1986

Empire of the Sun is based on the true story of an eleven-year-old British boy in China during World War II. To cast the lead role, Spielberg hired an unknown British child actor, Christian Bale. Under Spielberg's direction, Bale turned in a heartbreaking and intense performance—the first of many in that fine actor's career. The director and his crew spent three weeks in China shooting **exteriors** for the film. Ten thousand local residents were employed as extras for an amazing sequence in which residents flee as the Japanese army occupies Shanghai. Pre-war cars, Japanese tanks, and airplanes had to be flown to the location. Determined as always to be authentic, Spielberg spent $35 million making *Empire.*

The film, which ran over two-and-a-half hours, was released in December 1987. The reception from critics and audiences alike was lukewarm, but many Spielberg fans say this film is among Spielberg's best. It was also Spielberg's first serious attempt to film an intense subject from his childhood, World War II.

FAILURE AND SUCCESS

Meanwhile, things had changed at home. Spielberg's marriage was falling apart. His and Irving's careers had put them on different tracks, and there were other people in both their lives. As he had done before, Steven turned to work to help him get through during this unhappy period. He had decided to make another *Indiana Jones* film, his third. Again, Harrison Ford starred in the film, joined by Sean Connery as his comical, adventurous father. As a father himself, though, Spielberg was having a rough time. In May 1989, Spielberg and Irving divorced—sadly, but amicably. They agreed to share custody of their son, Max.

Indiana Jones and the Last Crusade opened in 2,327 theaters across the United States on May 24, 1989. The film broke box-office records for earnings its first weekend, taking in almost $47 million. Despite its success, the unhappy Spielberg kept himself busy by directing another picture.

Always was a remake of the 1944 romance, *A Guy Named Joe.* Spielberg cast Richard Dreyfuss, Holly Hunter, and John Goodman in the remake. Legendary actress Audrey Hepburn, in her last film appearance, played an angel. *Always* opened just before Christmas in 1989. The reviews were not good, and the film did badly at the box office.

A SECOND MARRIAGE

Spielberg might have been depressed about the failure of *Always,* but he wasn't. His personal life was looking up. He had resumed his relationship with actress Kate Capshaw, and they were getting serious. They had picked up where they left off five years earlier. Capshaw provided the stability that Spielberg needed. She was a woman who knew her own mind and settled for nothing less than a full commitment. Their relationship slowly deepened, and finally, on October 12, 1991, they were married.

During the time leading up to the marriage, Spielberg had been directing *Hook,* a spin-off of *Peter Pan.* He recalls, "I'd always loved and felt a connection to 'Peter Pan.' I actually directed 'Peter Pan' in high school on stage, so I knew the original well." In the film, Peter, played by Robin Williams, has grown up to become a selfish business tycoon and an absent father. Called to London on business, Peter takes his wife and children back to his childhood home. In a scene in Peter's old bedroom, Spielberg uses his visual trademark—a radiant light outside a window—to signal his audience that a magical experience awaits. Peter's old enemy, Captain Hook, kidnaps the children, and Peter returns to Neverland to rescue them. In the process, Peter is transformed into a man some might say resembles Spielberg—a devoted, loving father who remembers the magic of his childhood.

> **"I'd always loved and felt a connection to 'Peter Pan.'"**

Spielberg cast Dustin Hoffman as Captain Hook, Julia Roberts as Tinkerbell, Bob Hoskins as Smee, and Maggie Smith as a grown-up Wendy. It took nine stages to film *Hook.* The eventual cost of filming was between $60 million and $80 million. A *Variety* reviewer claims the film is "messy and undisciplined." Nevertheless, *Hook* made money, grossing $288 million worldwide.

Spielberg and Kate Capshaw

Spielberg didn't worry too much about *Hook*. With the strong support of his new wife, he threw himself wholeheartedly into a new project. The topic was dinosaurs.

JURASSIC PARK

In *Jurassic Park,* a wealthy businessman builds a theme park stocked with flesh-eating dinosaurs created by genetic cloning. In the park, the dinosaurs are separated from the public by an electric fence. Before the park opens to the public, its founder invites his grandchildren and some scientists to see it first. Everything goes haywire, however, when a computer failure shuts off the electricity, and the fence meant to separate the prehistoric beasts from the spectators is knocked down by a gigantic *Tyrannosaurus rex (T. rex)* dinosaur. All the dinosaurs escape, and horror and havoc follow. The children, in particular, endure one narrow escape after another. Thrill follows thrill as the humans do battle with the dinosaurs. During the harrowing climax, some characters are eaten alive, but the children and lead characters escape back to civilization.

As with *Jaws* and *E.T.*, Spielberg's major problem was creating the creatures. His dilemma pushed Spielberg into becoming knowledgeable about computers. This field had been his father's,

*Spielberg behind the camera during the
filming of* Jurassic Park

and Spielberg had always shied away from it. His
fear may have been reflected in the film. When
one of the scientists in the film learns that the
security system is computer operated, he responds,
"I hate computers."

Spielberg did not, however, begin with computers as his major tool. Rather, he went back to
the technology he had used in *Jaws.* His hope was

that the technology of building mechanical monsters had improved since then. He hired creature designer Stan Winston to build large, mechanically operated dinosaurs that were supposed to be much more technically advanced than the shark of two decades before. Phil Tippett was going to design some miniature go-motion dinosaurs. Almost as an afterthought, Spielberg decided to back up Winston and Tippett's work with some computer animation by Industrial Light & Magic (ILM), George Lucas's company. The man in charge of the animation was effects supervisor Dennis Muren.

One day Muren casually remarked to Spielberg that he could use computer graphics to create lifelike, full-size dinosaurs. Spielberg was dubious. He told Muren to prove it. Muren did just that. "He went out and proved it," Spielberg remembers. "I'd never seen movement this smooth outside of looking at *National Geographic* documentaries." When Spielberg showed the computer-generated dinosaurs to Tippett, the designer of miniatures gulped and said, "I think I'm extinct." (Spielberg gave actor Jeff Goldblum a similar line in the movie when he first sees the theme-park dinosaurs.)

While expensive models of *Tyrannosaurus, Brachiosaurus, Triceratops, Velociraptor,* and others were used for the shots of close-up conflict with the actors, most of the prehistoric beasts seen in

Jurassic Park were computer generated. Indeed, the impact of the Computer Generated Imagery (CGI) on Spielberg was so great that it led him to change the ending of *Jurassic Park*. Originally, he had planned a struggle between *Velociraptors*. He changed the ending to bring back *T. rex* in a blood-curdling, all-CGI rampage. It thrilled many viewers to the point of screaming and hiding their eyes. Technology had made the terror more real than anything seen on the screen before.

The genius of the team behind it—Muren, Tippett, Winston, and Michael Lantieri—was recognized when they won Oscars for visual effects. *Jurassic Park* also earned Oscars in the categories of Sound and Sound Effects Editing.

The film was released just in time for summer vacation in 1993. It had a PG-13 rating and was obviously aimed at older children. Parents protested that the terror generated by the film was too intense for young audiences. Some mental health professionals disagreed, claiming that children would distinguish the fantasy from the reality and come to terms with their fears. Spielberg said, "I think children are

"I think children are more traumatized by . . . a movie about child abuse or a movie about murder."

more traumatized by . . . a movie about child abuse or a movie about murder." He believed that while the images might be scary, the fear was only entertainment, and young viewers would recognize that.

Jurassic Park was the hit of the summer of 1993. At the box office, the film grossed more than $950 million worldwide. *Jurassic Park* passed *Star Wars* as the highest-grossing movie up to that time. *Jurassic Park* generated nearly $3 billion in ticket sales, video and television sales, merchandising, and other revenue sources. *The Los Angeles Times* estimated that Spielberg earned almost $300 million from *Jurassic Park.*

With some exceptions, the reviews were good. Although many thought the characters were cardboard cutouts, most critics applauded the dazzling special effects and rousing, relentless pace that characterizes Spielberg's style. Film critic Leonard Maltin wrote, "Slam-bang thriller delivers the goods with action, suspense, and hair-raising chills, plus the most astonishing special effects of this nature in cinema history: the dinosaurs seem *alive.*" *Time* magazine critic Richard Corliss noted, "For dinosaurs to rule the earth again, the monsters needed majesty as well as menace. And Spielberg got it all right." The young people who flocked to see the film obviously agreed.

CHAPTER ELEVEN

SCHINDLER'S LIST

In 1993, while Steven Spielberg was finishing up work on *Jurassic Park*, he was already deeply involved in the film that would bring him widespread acclaim. Based on the book by Thomas Keneally, *Schindler's List* tells the real-life story of Oskar Schindler. He was a German manufacturer who prevented many Jews from being murdered in Auschwitz—a Nazi concentration camp during World War II. This film put Spielberg in touch with the Jewish heritage he had never really known as a child.

He had never paid much attention to that identity, but Spielberg's wife, Kate Capshaw, says that he "rediscovered his Judaism when he had a family and realized he had something to pass on to them." Capshaw had converted to Judaism, and the children that they were to have together would be raised Jewish, as was his first son, Max.

Capshaw was pregnant with their son, Sasha, when the Spielbergs went to Poland to make arrangements to shoot *Schindler's List.*

CASTING THE LEADS

There are three main characters in the film: Schindler, Itzhak Stern, and Amon Goeth. Ambitious Schindler lavishly entertains Nazis, bribing them to let him open an enamelware plant in Krakow, Poland. He staffs it with Jewish workers, selected by Stern—a Jewish accountant and go-between for Schindler. Goeth is the sadistic, half-mad commandant of the nearby concentration camp. Schindler pays Goeth to release 1,100 Jewish workers into his custody.

Thinking about casting Schindler, Spielberg remembered a young Irish actor—Liam Neeson— who had auditioned for a role in *Empire of the Sun.* Impressed by him, Spielberg had told Neeson, "We're going to do something special someday." Now the tall, imposing actor with the commanding yet quiet manner seemed a natural to play Schindler. Neeson got the part. Oscar-winner Ben Kingsley played Stern. Ralph Fiennes, a British actor who was then unknown to American audiences, portrayed Nazi monster Goeth.

Spielberg had decided that the film must be shot in Poland and, wherever possible, at the loca-

*Spielberg directs Liam Neeson during the
filming of* Schindler's List.

tions where historical events had actually
occurred. He intended to begin inside Auschwitz.
However, the World Jewish Congress, which
administers the camp, denied him permission to
shoot there. Forced to compromise, Spielberg constructed a mirror image of Auschwitz just outside
its barbed-wire fence and shot the concentration-
camp scenes there.

THE LITTLE GIRL IN THE RED COAT

One of Spielberg's big problems was how to show why the amoral Schindler, who at first is only interested in making a profit off the Jews, becomes their savior. This change had to be demonstrated dramatically on the screen. Spielberg solved it with a long sequence, so powerful that it is already being studied in film schools.

In the scene, Schindler and one of his mistresses are out horseback riding when they pause at the top of a hill with a clear view of the Jewish quarter in the city below. Looking down, they see Nazi soldiers rounding up Jewish citizens. The scene, like the rest of the movie, is shot in black-and-white. However, one little girl wears a red coat. The camera follows her as she runs through the twisting streets trying to evade the Nazis. The camera cuts back and forth between her and Schindler's face as he observes the inhumanity of the roundup. Here, Neeson confirms Spielberg's judgment in casting him. Without dialogue, his face reveals the reaction of a man whose morality is dawning before his eyes. From this point forward, the film shows Schindler diverting his energy and money from profit and pleasure to risking his life to save the Jews in his custody.

Although *Schindler's List* might seem to be totally different from Spielberg's other films, the

> "What binds my films together is the concept of loneliness and isolation and being pursued by all the forces of character and nature. That comes from who I was and how I was raised."

director sees a connection. Spielberg said, "What binds my films together is the concept of loneliness and isolation and being pursued by all the forces of character and nature. That comes from who I was and how I was raised."

AT LONG LAST—OSCAR

Schindler's List opened in December 1993. The film ran three hours and fifteen minutes—a long time to sit through a movie about a subject as grim as the Holocaust. However, most viewers were quiet, attentive, and respectfully approving. Similarly, most critics praised the film. In *The New Yorker,* Terrence Rafferty wrote that *Schindler's List* was "the finest, fullest dramatic film ever made about the Holocaust." *Macleans'* reviewer called it "an undeniably powerful drama" and praised Spielberg for passing the lessons of the Holocaust on to future generations. A German newspaper recommended, "Everybody should see this film."

The picture won both the New York and Los Angeles Film Critic Awards. It received twelve Academy Award nominations and won eight Oscars. Spielberg walked off with his first two Oscar statues: one as Best Director and one as the producer of the film, which won Best Picture of

On March 21, 1994, Spielberg proudly shows off his two Oscars for Schindler's List.

1993. After being nominated by the Academy three times (for his direction of *Close Encounters, Raiders,* and *E.T.*) without ever winning, Spielberg finally won on March 21, 1994. Five years later, in an interview in *Entertainment Weekly,* Spielberg's passion for *Schindler's List* was still

——————

"I've never been more careful about telling a story in my entire career."

——————

evident. He said, "I've never been more careful about telling a story in my entire career. And it was very emotionally difficult to make. But it was nothing compared to what the survivors had to endure—the price we paid to get the film made was just a drop of water compared to the lakes and lakes of tears over the last half century. It's the most personal film I've ever made—and probably ever will make."

CHAPTER TWELVE

THE AMISTAD CONTROVERSIES

Following *Schindler's List,* the satisfactions of Spielberg's family life kept him from immediately taking on another directing project. He was busy raising a family of seven children with Kate Capshaw. Spielberg says, "I was Mr. Carpool. We had breakfast and dinner together every day. It's full-time work, because every one of our kids is a leader. Seven leaders, no followers." Spielberg's children are: Jessica Capshaw, Kate Capshaw's daughter from an earlier marriage; Max, Spielberg's son by Amy Irving; three children by Capshaw—Sasha, Sawyer, and Destry; and two adopted African-American children, Theo and Mikaela. The family lives in Pacific Palisades, California, and East Hampton, New York.

To have more time with his family, Spielberg concentrated on producing instead of directing from 1994 to 1997. He was the executive producer

In 1996, Spielberg shoots The Lost World, *the sequel to* Jurassic Park.

of *Casper, Twister, Men in Black,* and *The Lost World: Jurassic Park.* In this last film, he eased back into directing.

The Lost World picks up where *Jurassic Park* left off and focuses on a second island populated by dinosaurs. *The Lost World* earned mixed reviews when it opened in May 1997. One criticism was that most of the dinosaur scenes take place at night—making them scarier but also murkier. Otherwise, the special effects were highly praised. Joseph McBride describes the sequel as "a beautifully crafted series of nightmarish set pieces with no other goal in mind than to scare and delight the audience." On the other hand, film critic Roger Ebert said, "You sense that although much effort was lavished on the special effects, Spielberg's interest in the story was perfunctory." Still, the film was a huge box-office success, grossing $229 million at the box office. A practical businessman, Spielberg admits that the main reason he made *The Lost World* was that he knew it would earn him a lot of money.

THE EARLY PROTESTS

While he was shooting *The Lost World,* Spielberg was preparing to direct *Amistad,* the story of a slave mutiny on an 1839 Spanish slave ship. When the U.S. Coast Guard captured the ship, the mutineers were imprisoned while their fate was decided. People questioned whether or not the slaves were "property" to be returned to Spain or human beings free to return to Africa. The controversy pitted slaveholders against abolitionists—people who fought to free slaves. In 1841, the cause of the mutineers was successfully argued before the U.S. Supreme Court by former President John Quincy Adams, and the slaves were "declared to be free."

From the first, Spielberg had problems with the project. Prominent African-Americans of

Spielberg and Debbie Allen (center) in rehearsal for Amistad

widely varying political views—including Louis Farrakhan, Professor Cornel West, and Spike Lee—protested that no white director could do justice to the subject of slavery. When it became known that Spielberg had cast top star Anthony Hopkins in the role of John Quincy Adams, many people believed that the movie would focus on whites, while black slaves would simply move the plot along. Their concern was that Spielberg would focus on the trial and present the mutineers as victims rather than as Africans who had fought and died for their freedom.

THE PLAGIARISM SUIT

Despite the protests, Spielberg went ahead with the project. He hired renowned **cinematographer** Janusz Kaminski, who had also photographed *Schindler's List,* to ensure the stark mood he wanted to portray the horrors of slavery. The cast included Morgan Freeman, Stellan Skarsgard, Matthew McConaughey, and Anna Paquin. The most powerful, dominant role went to an unknown actor named Djimon Hounsou who played Cinque, the non-English-speaking leader of the revolt.

Shooting proceeded through the summer of 1997. *Amistad* was scheduled for release on December 10, 1997. It was being edited on October 17 when award-winning African-American author Barbara Chase-Riboud filed a suit claiming that *Amistad* had **plagiarized** material from her 1989 book, *Echo of Lions.* She asked for $10 million in damages.

In 1988, Jacqueline Kennedy Onassis, Ms. Chase-Riboud's editor at Doubleday, had submitted *Echo of Lions* to Amblin Entertainment, Spielberg's production company, for consideration as a movie. Amblin had turned it down. Now Ms. Chase-Riboud alleged certain characters had been stolen from her book. She requested an injunction to keep the film from opening on schedule.

"GIVE US FREE!"

In court, Spielberg's company said the *Amistad* script was based on history and on the book *Black Mutiny*, which had been published thirty-six years before *Echo of Lions*. Spielberg's company had bought the rights to *Black Mutiny*. *Amistad* screenwriter David Franzoni testified that he had never read *Echo of Lions*. Ms. Chase-Riboud's request to stop the film from opening was denied.

Accusations followed that Ms. Chase-Riboud had plagiarized material from *Black Mutiny* and another book in *Echo of Lions*. She denied the charges, but on February 9, 1998, two months after *Amistad* opened, she dropped her suit against Spielberg's company. She also praised both the film and Spielberg's courage in making it.

When *Amistad* was shown in theaters, however, it divided the audiences, especially the African-American community. Some felt that Hopkins' long speech and the political sidelights covered in the film detracted from the story of the slaves' heroism and ordeal. Others thought that Spielberg had dramatized the horrors of slavery better than any other filmmaker. Many viewers were thrilled to the point of tears when Cinque stands up in court and repeatedly shouts out his powerful demand that the dignity of his people be recognized: "Give us free!" he thunders. "Give us free!"

Besides showing *Amistad* to hundreds of high school students free of charge, Spielberg has supplied many schools around the country with an *Amistad* study guide and learning kit at no cost. Inevitably, this gesture has aroused controversy too. Both film critic Michael Medved and historian Earl C. Hutchinson have objected on the grounds that the film is a dramatization that takes liberties with the facts,

_____

"I have two [adopted] African-American children, and I wanted to leave something behind for them on a subject matter that they need to know about."

_____

and therefore, is not historically accurate. Debbie Allen, who shares production credits with Spielberg, dismissed the charges as "trying to denigrate once again the contribution of African people." Spielberg refused to comment on the criticisms, but he has discussed his reason for doing the film. He said, "I have two [adopted] African-American children, and I wanted to leave something behind for them on a subject matter that they need to know about."

CHAPTER THIRTEEN

WAR AND REMEMBRANCE

By the late 1990s, Steven Spielberg was clearly a different filmmaker and person from the young, punky dynamo who scared audiences with *Jaws* in 1975. His films now mixed "popcorn" entertainment, such as *Jurassic Park,* with sober, serious themes, such as *Schindler's List* and *Amistad.* No longer a shy loner, he was a happy family man. In addition to making great films, Spielberg began to concern himself with other ways he could help society.

He is the chairman of the Starbright Foundation, which has raised $40 million to provide online computer links to children's wards in hospitals. Spielberg often visits children in schools and hospitals, and he feels that the combination of entertainment and technology can help children heal. Those who know him best say his char-

Spielberg, Kate Capshaw, and two of their children,
Max and Theo, on a family outing in 1998

itable activities are an outgrowth of his feelings for his family.

He wants his children to know and appreciate their heritage. Spielberg affirms the importance of his children's heritages by financing educational projects that emphasize African-American history and Holocaust remembrance. In the fall of 1994, he gave part of his earnings from *Schindler's List* to establish the Righteous Persons Foundation. It has given $3 million to the United States Holocaust Memorial Museum, $1 million to New York City's Museum of Jewish Heritage, and $500,000 to the Fortunoff Video Archive for Holocaust Testimonies at Yale University. In 1999, the foundation gave the National Yiddish Book Center a grant of $500,000 to create a digital version of the center's collection—the Steven Spielberg Digital Library. These donations are only some examples of the more than $85 million that Spielberg has given to support Jewish culture and education.

THE SURVIVORS OF THE SHOAH VISUAL HISTORY FOUNDATION

The best known of Spielberg's philanthropies is the Survivors of the Shoah Visual History Foundation. He founded it in 1994 with an initial gift of $6 million, part of his profits from *Schindler's*

List. This nonprofit organization is dedicated to videotaping and preserving interviews of Holocaust survivors all over the world. The interviews have been conducted in 33 languages by a staff of 240, with the help of more than 3,800 volunteers worldwide. Eventually, the interviews will comprise the most comprehensive library of Holocaust survivor testimony ever assembled and will be used to teach racial, ethnic, and cultural tolerance. The Shoah database contains names and information about 50,000 Holocaust survivors around the world. Taped interviews with some of them were used to produce *Survivors: Testimonies of the Holocaust*, a CD-ROM disk for use in high schools.

Spielberg devotes a great deal of time to his Shoah Foundation activities, and sometimes he combines them with his role as a movie producer. In 1998, he was executive producer for the Shoah Visual History Foundation on a full-length Holocaust documentary, *The Last Days*. It is described as "the story of five remarkable people whose strength and will to live represent the extraordinary power of the human spirit." The film won the Academy Award for Best Documentary of 1998.

SAVING PRIVATE RYAN

While devoting energy to his philanthropic enterprises, Spielberg continues to work on films. Following *Amistad,* he acted as producer on *Deep Impact* and *The Mask of Zorro.* Also in 1998, he both produced and directed *Saving Private Ryan.*

Saving Private Ryan was inspired by a 1943 real-life incident in which five brothers, named Sullivan, were all killed during the same naval battle in World War II. In Spielberg's film, three brothers named Ryan are killed in battle. A decision is made to remove a fourth Ryan brother (played by Matt Damon) from combat during the fighting in Normandy following the D-Day invasion of 1944. A squad led by Captain Miller, played by Tom Hanks, is assigned to find Private Ryan and bring him back to be shipped home. The assignment pulls the squad deeper and deeper into battle. When they finally find him, he refuses to go with them because his undermanned outfit has been assigned to defend a bridge. The squad stays with Ryan and is wiped out defending the bridge, but Private Ryan survives.

As with other Spielberg films, *Saving Private Ryan* stirred up controversy. Spielberg said that he considers it an anti-war film. It opens with twenty-seven minutes of what *New Yorker* critic Hendrik Hertzberg calls "the most harrowing depiction of battle ever put on screen." The film climaxes with another long battle scene that is almost as horrifying as the opening. These scenes were shot with hand-held cameras, so they are held low, as if combat photographers are crouch-

Spielberg directs Tom Hanks during the filming of the opening sequence of Saving Private Ryan.

ing to avoid the shells landing around them. These two sequences, especially the opening one, propel the viewer into the terrifying experience of being a combat soldier. Rather than depicting combat as a thrilling endeavor (as most Hollywood movies do), Spielberg wanted to convey the horror, pain, and fear that he remembered from the stories that veterans had told him when he was young. Yet, some critics say that the story between these two scenes is, in many ways, just as standard as the plots in war movies that Hollywood has churned out for decades.

HONORING HIS FATHER

Top *New York Times* film critic Janet Maslin hailed *Saving Private Ryan* as "a soberly magnificent new war film" and "the finest war movie of our time." Despite the bloody battle scenes, *New Yorker* critic Hertzberg concluded that the film "honors the dead and the survivors of Normandy." Most of the reviews were glowing. Some who criticized the film thought that the scenes of violence were too realistic, particularly for young audiences.

Spielberg does not disagree. He says, "I tried to be as brutally honest as I could." He has said that he doesn't think the film is suitable for viewing by anyone under the age of fifteen. He has urged parents to keep their young children away from it. He hasn't permitted his oldest son, Max, to see it yet. Ironically, many of the soldiers who

"I tried to be as brutally honest as I could."

Spielberg accepts his third Oscar—for directing
Saving Private Ryan—*on March 21, 1999.*

died on the beaches and in the hedgerows of Normandy were only seventeen and eighteen years old.

Is *Saving Private Ryan* an anti-war film, or does its depiction of the close comradeship of men in combat glorify the sacrifice of life? Viewers will have to decide for themselves. Their decisions will be based on whether or not the horrors of war portrayed so graphically in the film are outweighed by the bravery and sacrifice of the characters.

Saving Private Ryan received eleven Academy Award nominations, including Best Picture, Best Director, Best Actor (Tom Hanks), and Best Cinematography. It won five Oscars, including one for cinematographer Janusz Kaminski—a tribute to the graphic battle shots—and one for Spielberg as Best Director. (It did not, however, win Best Picture. *Shakespeare in Love* won that award.)

"I really wanted this," Spielberg said as he accepted the Best Director award. He paid tribute to the families who lost sons in World War II. Then he turned to his father sitting in the audience. "Thank you for showing me that there is honor in looking back and respecting the past," he told his father. He held up the Oscar statuette and added, "This is for you."

AWARDS AND ACHIEVEMENTS

In addition to his Oscars, Spielberg has received numerous awards and honors—too many to list completely. Along with other awards mentioned throughout this biography, he received the Lifetime Achievement Award from the American Film Institute in 1995. He has won three Daytime Emmy Awards for his animated programs, *Pinky and the Brain* and *Tiny Toon Adventures*. Film and entertainment journals often mention him in their achievement lists. In October 1997, *Entertainment Weekly* called him the most powerful person in the entertainment industry. Two years later, in its November 5, 1999, edition, *Entertainment Weekly* named Spielberg the fourth most important entertainer—and the most important filmmaker—of the century. Spielberg's high ranking on this list is, in part, because he has directed six films of the top twenty-five all-time box-office hits—*E.T., Jurassic Park, Jaws, Raiders of the Lost Ark, Lost World,* and *Schindler's List.*

DREAMWORKS SKG

As artistically successful as Spielberg has been, he is just as good a businessman. In 1994, Spielberg joined with film executive Jeffrey Katzenberg and musical industry genius David Geffen to form the first new Hollywood film studio since the late 1970s. The company, DreamWorks SKG (the initials standing for the last names of the three partners), produces films, TV programming, interactive software, and records.

On Oct. 12, 1994, Jeffrey Katzenberg (left), Spielberg (center), and David Geffen (right) announce the founding of Dreamworks SKG.

DreamWorks has provided Spielberg with the opportunity to use his creative talents in other media and expand his business interests. For example, DreamWorks Interactive produced a video game, *The Lost World*, based on the film. Fully orchestrated with dinosaur sounds and 3-D animation, it offers 30 levels of game play based on creatures created for the film. An avid video game player, Spielberg drops by DreamWorks

Interactive almost every day to play new games—often bringing his children.

Although he takes time out for fun, Spielberg still takes his interest in DreamWorks seriously, especially its movies. The film and television divisions have had their successes, such as *Spin City, Saving Private Ryan,* and *American Beauty,* and their failures—such as *In Dreams* and *Small Soldiers.* DreamWorks is also known for producing the computer-animated *Antz* and the full-length cartoon film *Prince of Egypt,* both released in 1998. *Antz,* with Woody Allen providing the voice for the lead, was a smash hit. *Prince of Egypt* did not fare as well, but it did not lose money. Although Spielberg is a partner in DreamWorks, he is not directly involved in every film the company releases.

COMING ATTRACTIONS

Meanwhile, Steven Spielberg moves on to other projects—some with companies other than DreamWorks. As this book is being written, Spielberg is producing *The Martian Chronicles,* which premieres in 2000. He plans to direct another sci-fi film, *Minority Report,* starring Tom Cruise. This film is supposed to be released in 2000. Although he once said he'd never do another *Jurassic Park* film, Spielberg is working on *Jurassic Park 3,* scheduled for release in 2001. Also that year, he plans to direct an adaptation of the book *Memoirs of a Geisha* and *Indiana Jones IV*. He is already lining up more than sixty projects besides these, including a computer-animated version of *The Cat in the Hat* and a biography of Charles Lindbergh. He concludes, "I don't have enough time in a lifetime to tell all the stories I want to tell."

"I don't have enough time in a lifetime to tell all the stories I want to tell."

His moviegoing fans should be reassured. The future is bright. The genius of Steven Spielberg is still a work in progress.

CHRONOLOGY

1946	Steven Allan Spielberg is born on December 18.
1952	The Spielberg family moves to Haddon Township, New Jersey.
1957	The Spielberg family moves to Phoenix, Arizona.
1958	Twelve-year-old Steven takes his first pictures with his father's 8-mm movie camera.
1958–1960	Steven makes short movies, *Gunsmog* and *Battle Squad,* using classmates as actors.
1963–1964	Steven makes *Firelight*, a 140-minute long sci-fi film. It is shown in a local theater.
1964	The Spielberg family moves to Saratoga, California.
1965	Steven's parents divorce; he graduates from high school.
1967–68	Spielberg makes the short film *Amblin'*.
1969	*Amblin'* wins a prize at an Atlanta Film Festival, and Spielberg is signed to seven-year contract by Universal Studios. Spielberg directs a "Night Gallery" TV segment starring Joan Crawford.

1971	*Duel,* a made-for-TV movie directed by Spielberg, airs on November 13.
1973	*Duel* is shown in theaters abroad, wins festival prizes, and gains a cult following.
1974	Spielberg's first movie for the big screen, *The Sugarland Express,* is released.
1975	*Jaws,* Spielberg's first box-office smash hit, is released. He becomes a millionaire.
1976	Spielberg meets Amy Irving, falls in love, and starts production on *Close Encounters of the Third Kind.*
1977	*Close Encounters* is released. Jessica Capshaw, Kate's daughter, is born.
1979	Spielberg directs *1941;* it flops. Spielberg and Irving end their affair.
1981	Spielberg directs *Raiders of the Lost Ark;* it earns $310 million in its first year of release.
1982	*E.T. the Extra-Terrestrial,* directed by Spielberg, is released and widely acclaimed.
1983	Spielberg begins work on *Indiana Jones and the Temple of Doom* and becomes involved with Kate Capshaw. Spielberg becomes re-involved with Amy Irving.
1985	Spielberg changes pace with *The Color Purple* and stirs up controversy. Spielberg's and Irving's son Max is born on June 13, 1985. Spielberg and Irving marry on November 27. They are on their honeymoon when *The Color Purple* opens to mixed reviews.
1987	Spielberg receives the Irving Thalberg Memorial Award. Spielberg's *Empire of the Sun* opens to mixed reviews.
1988	Kate Capshaw adopts Theo; later, Spielberg adopts him too.

1989	Irving and Spielberg divorce. *Indiana Jones and the Last Crusade* opens and is a big success. He directs *Always,* a failure with critics and at the box office. Spielberg resumes his relationship with Kate Capshaw.
1990	Spielberg's and Capshaw's son Sasha is born on May 14.
1991	Capshaw and Spielberg marry on October 12; he directs *Hook.*
1992	Sawyer Spielberg is born on March 11, 1992.
1993	Spielberg directs *Jurassic Park.* It grosses more than $950 million worldwide.
1994	*Schindler's List* wins eight Oscars, including Best Picture and Best Director.
1996	Spielberg and Capshaw adopt Mikaela George in February; Destry Allyn is born on December 1, 1996
1997	Spielberg directs *The Lost World: Jurassic Park.* It gets mixed reviews but scores at the box office. Amid controversy, criticism, and claims of plagiarism Spielberg directs *Amistad.*
1998	*Saving Private Ryan* breaks new ground with uniquely realistic war footage.
1999	*Saving Private Ryan* wins five Oscars, including one for Spielberg as Best Director.

SELECTED FILMOGRAPHY

FILMS DIRECTED BY STEVEN SPIELBERG

"Eyes" (Segment of TV series *Night Gallery*)	1969
Duel	1971
The Sugarland Express	1974
Jaws	1975
Close Encounters of the Third Kind	1977
1941	1979
Raiders of the Lost Ark	1981
E.T. the Extra-Terrestrial	1982
Kick the Can (Segment of *Twilight Zone: The Movie*)	1983
Indiana Jones and the Temple of Doom	1984
The Color Purple	1985
Empire of the Sun	1987
Always	1989
Indiana Jones and the Last Crusade	1989
Hook	1991
Jurassic Park	1993
Schindler's List	1993
The Lost World: Jurassic Park	1997
Amistad	1997
Saving Private Ryan	1998

Minority Report (in production)	2000
Memoirs of a Geisha (in production)	2001
Indiana Jones IV (in production)	2001

FILMS WRITTEN BY STEVEN SPIELBERG

Ace Eli & Rodger of the Skies (Story)	1973
Close Encounters of the Third Kind	1977
Poltergeist (Story)	1982
The Goonies (Story)	1985
What Lies Beneath (in production)	2000
Jurassic Park 3 (in production)	2001

GLOSSARY

anti-Semitic prejudiced against or hostile toward Jews

cinematographer a movie photographer

cliffhanger a suspenseful situation at the end of a chapter, a scene, or an episode

climax the point in a series of events that is of greatest intensity or effect, usually occurring near the end

composition the arrangement of parts or elements, as in an artistic work

cue cards poster-like cards that contain elements of an actor's lines

cut a transition in a film within a sequence. Cuts are made by uniting one strip of film to another

documentary a nonfiction motion picture usually filmed where history or an event took place and designed to depict the action and show why it was significant

edit to put together or cut out parts of a motion picture, videotape, or recording

executive producer the person who supervises and manages the making and public presentation of a play, film, television show, or other entertainment

exteriors   outside scenes, often shot on location
footage   the total amount of running feet of motion-picture film used
framing   one picture of a series on a length of film
long shot   a section of film that shows the main object at a considerable distance from the camera, presenting it in relation to its general surroundings (See also *shot*)
medium shot   a section of film that shows the object in relation to its immediate surroundings (See also *shot*)
overexposed   film that has been exposed to too much light
panning shot   a section of film taken with the camera moving to the right or left while its base remains fixed (See also *shot*)
perspective   a mental view of the relationships of the aspects of a subject to each other and to a whole
pilot   a television program that serves as the model of a series being considered for production by a network
plagiarize   to use and pass off as one's own the ideas or writings of another
retake   a second or later filming, photographing, or recording undertaken to improve upon the first
screenplay   the script for a motion picture
screenwriter   the person who writes the script for a motion picture
script   the text of a play, motion picture, or broadcast
serials   filmed adventure stories split up into fifteen- to twenty-minute chapters with cliffhanger endings
shot   what is recorded between the time a camera starts and the time it stops
sound stage   the part of a motion-picture studio in which a production is filmed
storyboards   cartoon-like pages showing how scenes are framed and cameras moved

studio   a room or building for motion-picture, television, or radio production

synagogue   a building or place of meeting for worship and religious instruction in the Jewish faith

Torah   the sacred scroll kept in a synagogue. It contains the first five books of the Bible

turret   a device on a camera that holds and rotates several lenses

A NOTE ON SOURCES

These primary sources were used in researching the background and career of Steven Spielberg: *Steven Spielberg: The Unauthorized Biography* by John Baxter (London: HarperCollins, 1996), *Steven Spielberg* by Bertram Knight (New York: Silver Burdett Press, 1998), *Steven Spielberg* by Philip M. Taylor (New York: Continuum, 1994), *Steven Spielberg: Creator of E. T.* by Tom Collins (Minneapolis: Dillon Press, 1983), *Steven Spielberg: Hollywood Filmmaker* by Virginia Meachum (Springfield, NJ: Enslow, 1996), and *The Films of Steven Spielberg* by Douglas Brode (New York: Carol, 1994).

For general information regarding the films of Steven Spielberg and his contemporaries, I relied on *Leonard Maltin's 1999 Movie & Video Guide* (New York: Plume Books, 1998), *Halliwell's Film Guide,* 6th Edition by Leslie Halliwell (New York: Charles Scribner's Sons, 1987) and *The Encyclopedia of Hollywood* by Scott and Barbara Siegel (New York: Facts on File, 1990). News stories, articles and reviews from various editions of *The New York Times, The Wall Street Journal, Business Week, Newsday, The Nation, The New Yorker, The Atlantic Monthly, Showbiz Today, Variety, Hollywood Reporter, Film Comment,* and *Premiere* were also used.

FOR MORE INFORMATION

BOOKS

Baxter, John. *Steven Spielberg: The Unauthorized Biography.* London: HarperCollins, 1996.

Brode, Douglas. *The Films of Steven Spielberg.* New York: Citadel, 1995.

Collins, Tom. *Steven Spielberg: Creator of E.T.* Minneapolis, MN: Dillon Press, 1983.

Ferber, Elizabeth. *Steven Spielberg.* Philadelphia: Chelsea House, 1996.

Knight, Bertram. *Steven Spielberg.* New York: Silver Burdett Press, 1998.

Loshitzky, Yosefa (Editor). *Spielberg's Holocaust.* Bloomington, IN: Indiana University Press, 1997.

McBride, Joseph. *Steven Spielberg: A Biography.* New York: Simon & Schuster, 1997.

Shay, Don & Duncan, Jody. *The Making of Jurassic Park.* New York: Ballantine, 1993.

Taylor, Derek. *The Making of Raiders of the Lost Ark.* New York: Ballantine, 1981.

Taylor, Philip M. *Steven Spielberg.* New York: Continuum, 1994.

CD-ROM

Spielberg, Steven. *Steven Spielberg's Director's Chair.*
Produced by DreamWorks Interactive, this CD-ROM puts the player in the director's chair. Spielberg introduces would-be directors to many phases of film production, including selecting camera angles, editing, scoring, and adding sound effects.

ORGANIZATIONS AND INTERNET RESOURCES

Amblin Entertainment
P.O. Box 8520
100 Universal City Plaza
Universal City, CA 91608
(818) 733-7000
Send fan mail to Spielberg at this address.

DreamWorks SKG
100 Universal City Plaza, Suite 601
Universal City, CA 91608
(310) 571-2222
http://www.dreamworks.com
Find out about the latest films produced by Spielberg's company. This site also includes links to DreamWorks Interactive and DreamWorks Records.

Entertainment Weekly Online
http://www.pathfinder.com/ew/
This journal's online site is particularly user friendly. Search under *Spielberg* for articles on the director.

The Internet Movie Database
http://www.imdb.com
Search this extensive site for information on movies and people in the film industry.

The Righteous Persons Foundation
1460 4th Street, Suite 212
Santa Monica, CA 90401
(310) 395-3599
This grant-making organization funds projects for Jewish youth, encourages Jewish learning, and promotes tolerance and inter-group relations.

The Starbright Foundation
1990 S. Bundy Drive, Suite 100
Los Angeles, CA 90025
(310) 442-1560
http://www.starbright.org
Students can go to this site to learn about the foundation's projects to help seriously ill children cope with their challenges. Spielberg is the foundation's chairman.

The Survivors of the Shoah Visual History Foundation
P.O. Box 3168
Los Angeles, CA 90078-3168
(818) 777-4673
http://www.vhf.org
At the foundation's home page, read about the organization's history and goals, the interview process, the production status of the interviews, and *The Last Days*. The site also includes links to related organizations.

INDEX

Italicized page numbers indicate illustrations.

ABOUT THE AUTHOR

Ted Gottfried has written more than fifty books, both fiction and nonfiction. His previous books for Franklin Watts include *Alan Turing: Architect of the Computer Age*; *Alexander Fleming: Discoverer of Penicillin*; *American Media*; *Eleanor Roosevelt: First Lady of the Twentieth Century*; and *James Baldwin: A Voice from Harlem*. Mr. Gottfried has taught writing at New York University, Baruch College, and other institutions. He and his wife, Harriet, live in New York City.